Brackenwood

Character Sketchbook

2002-2012

Adam Phillips

ISBN: 1481214454
ISBN-13: 978-1481214452

DEDICATION

Dedicated to all of Brackenwood's family, fans and supporters. Special thanks to the backers of the 2011 Dashkin Kickstarter campaign, without whom this sketchbook would not exist.

CONTENTS

INTRODUCTION

I unpacked a large box of old drawings recently and these were amongst them smudged, crumpled and in no particular order.

Most of the images in this book are scanned from those original drawings on paper, so they're mostly very loose sketches frequently accompanied by creases and scrub marks.

Generally, these were sketched as I was getting to know the character, so there's scant adherence to any 'model' as I experimented with proportions, poses, gestures and expressions.

BINGBONG

He was the start of it all. Bingbong was originally the central character of the series. However as the world of Brackenwood evolved around him, he became secondary, then later incidental to the story.

Even though he's no longer a main character, Bingbong will always have a place in the star line-up, as he represents that single spark of an idea from which all Brackenwood sprang.

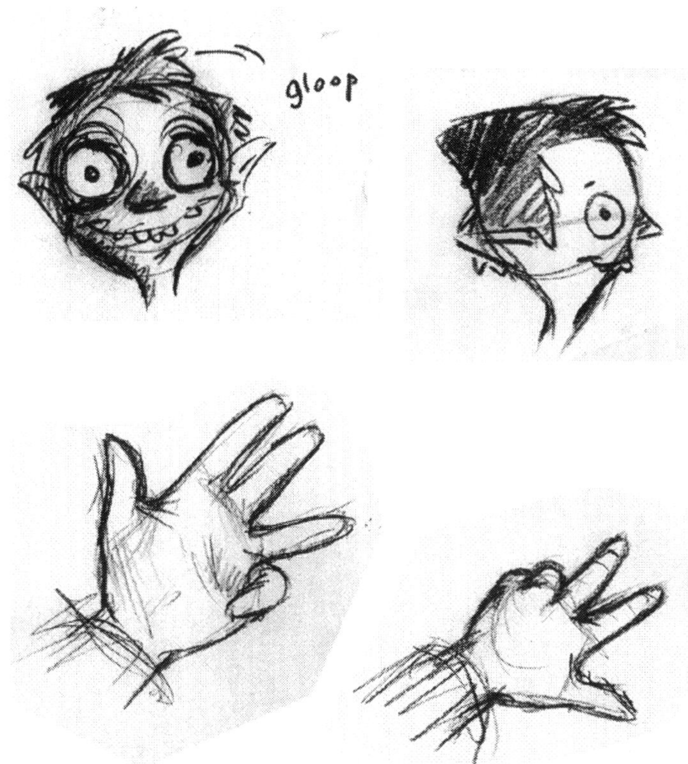
gloop

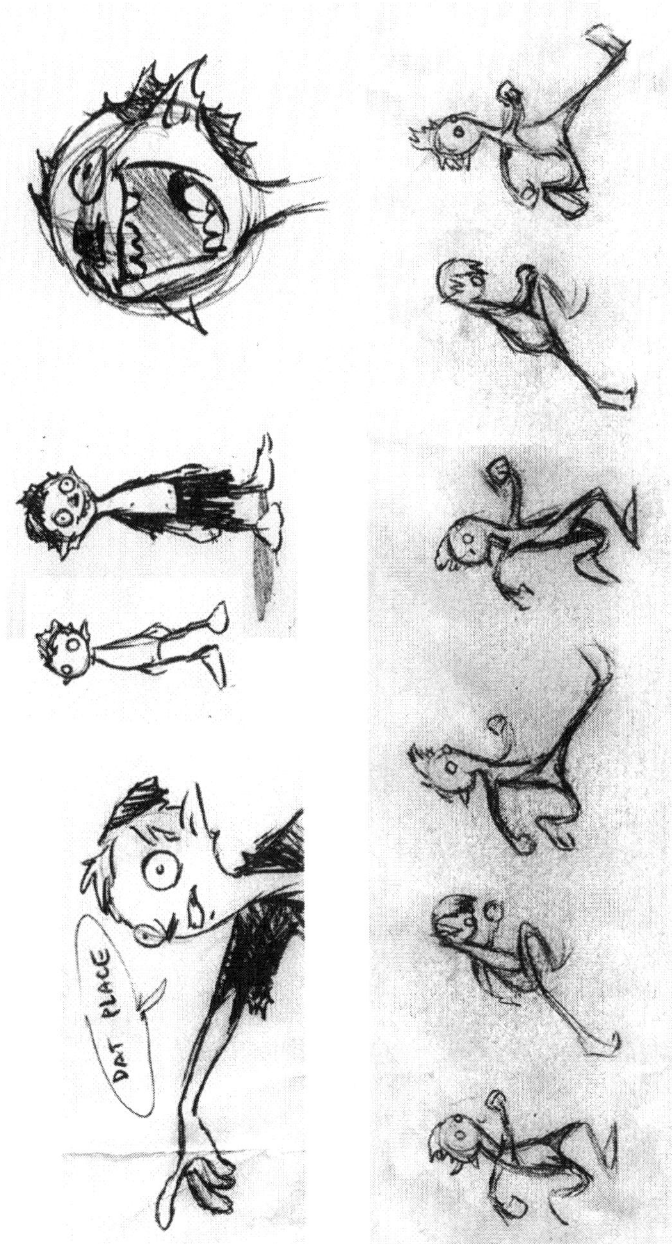
DAT PLACE

B
FFFF
try to help a butterfly back into its cocoon

DANCE

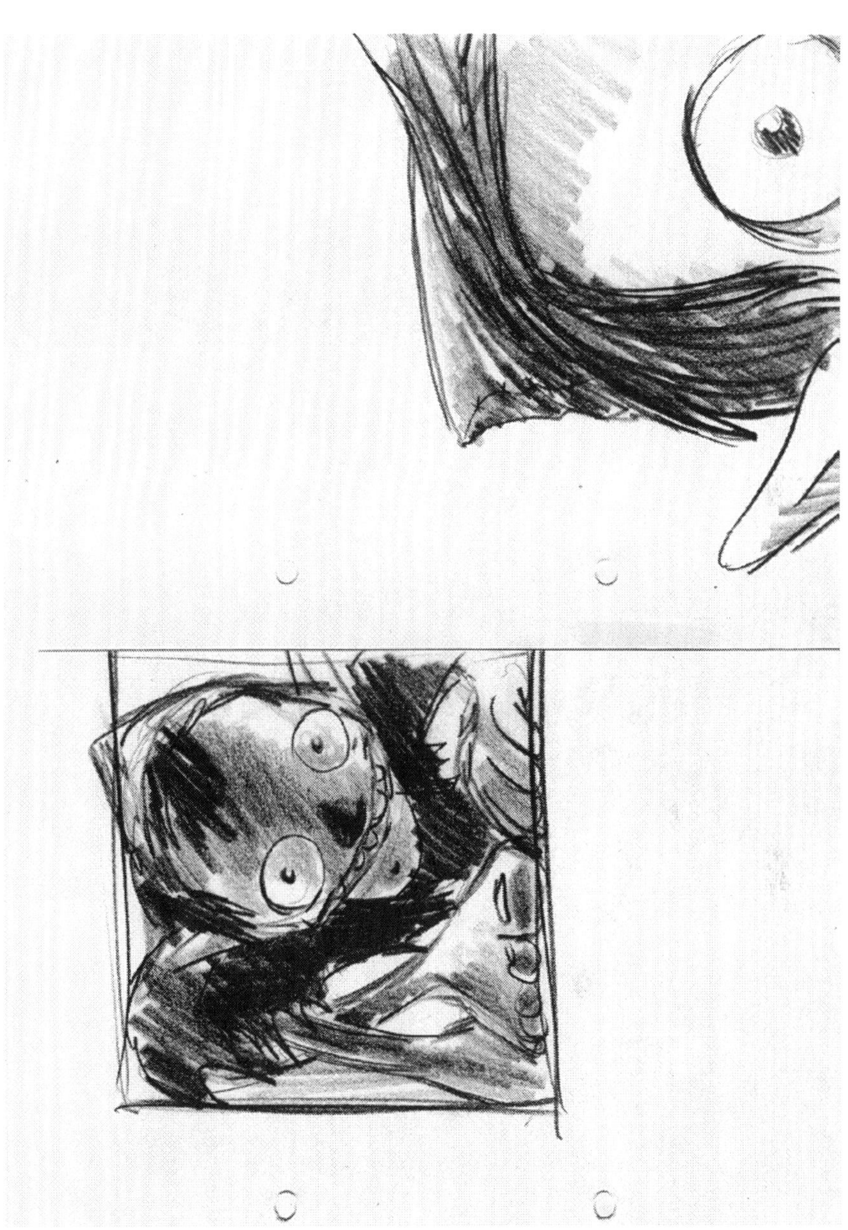

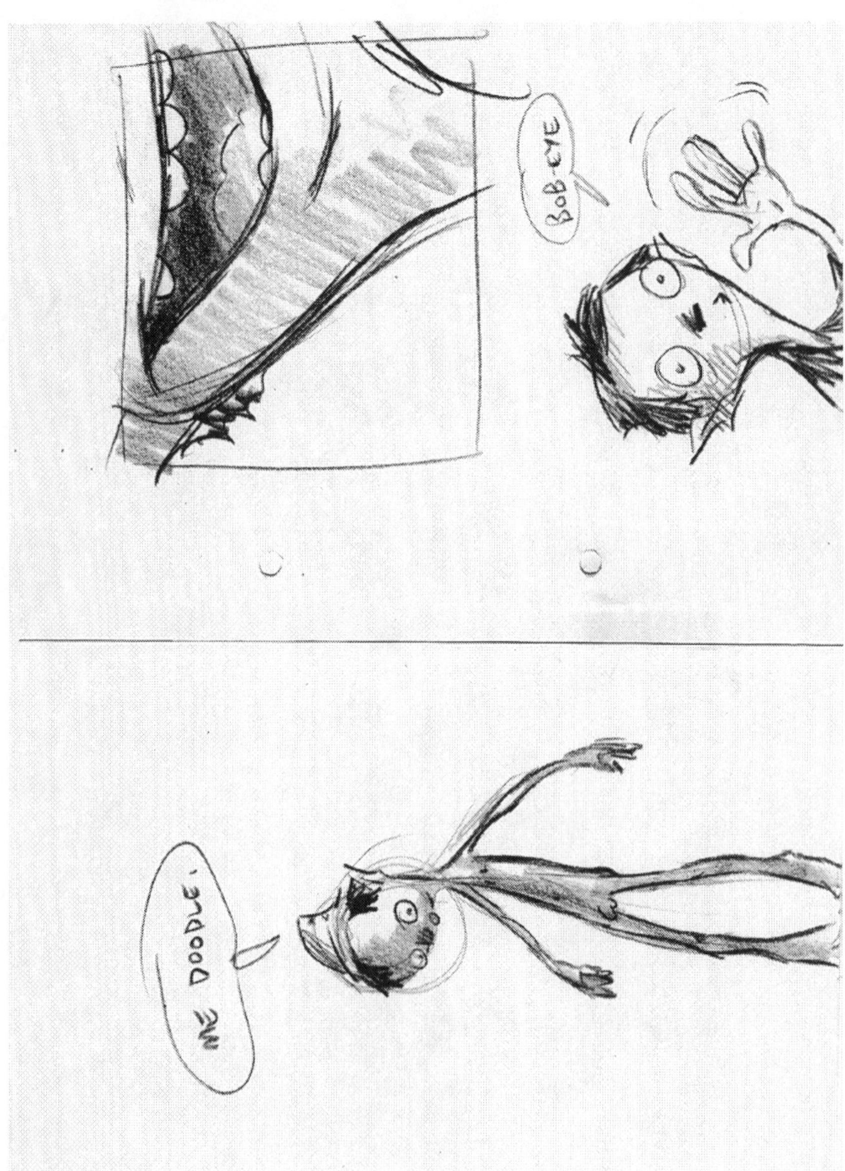
ME DOODLE.
BOB-EYE

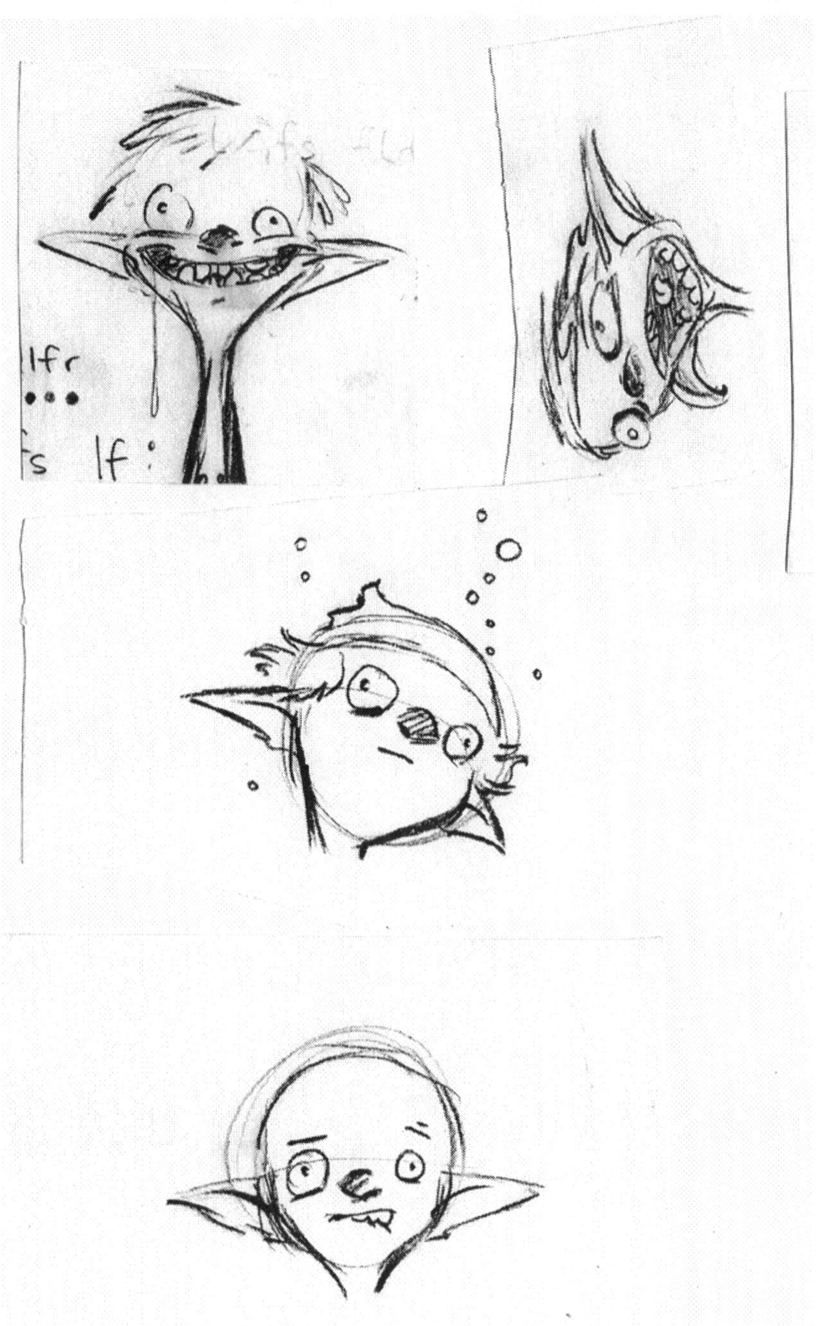

BITEY

Next to come along was Bitey. I created him especially to antagonise the loveable Bingbong. To be a despicable nemesis.

Originally named "Mortis", I couldn't seem to come up with an interesting face for him. One day in frustration, I scribbled over his head. Staring back at me from the page was the fur-faced character we know today. You can see that exact drawing and the moment of Bitey's birth just ahead on page 18.

I renamed him Bitey because I wanted a more fun and simple name with a slightly sinister undertone.

Most of my life I've been quite fond of the word "bitey" to describe nasty creatures. When I was a toddler, my mother would roll black thread into untidy little balls and tape them to the power outlets. Thinking they were spiders, I'd stare at them from a safe distance, point and say "ooh, bitey!".

Incidentally, this is also why my first domain name was oohbitey.com and featured a spider as the logo.

GGRRRAAAAA

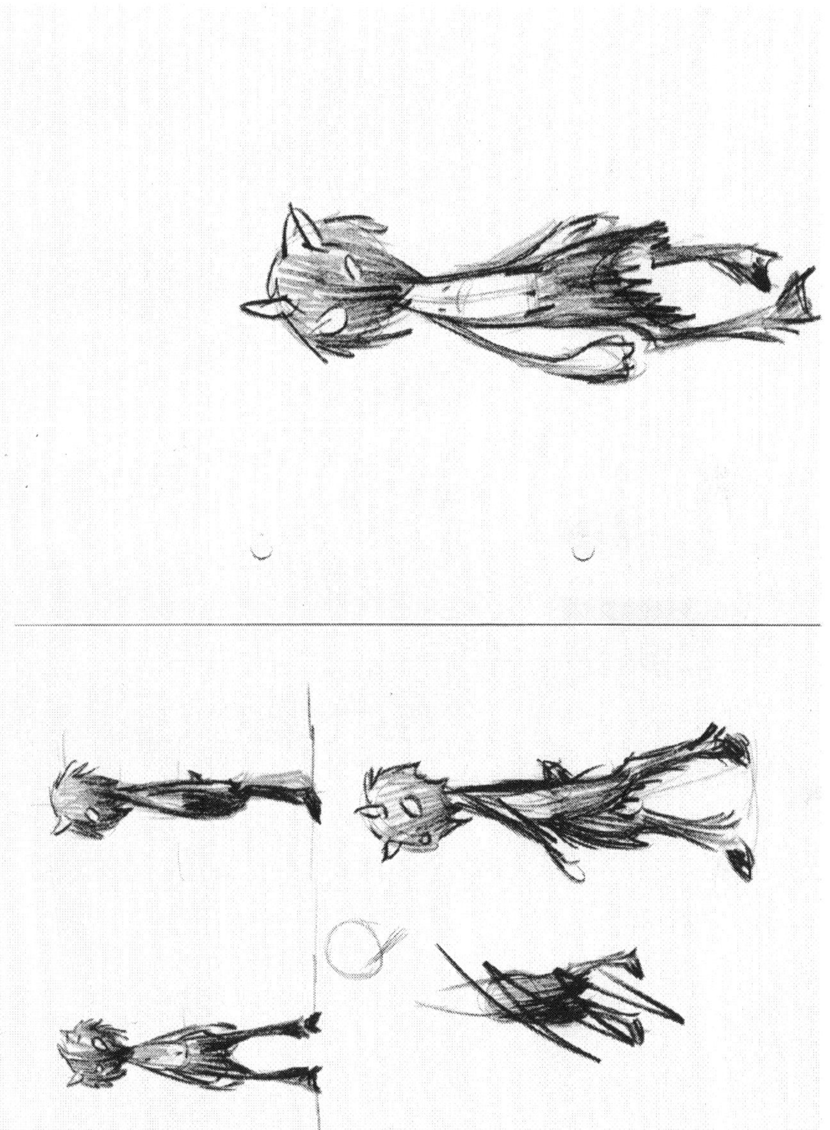

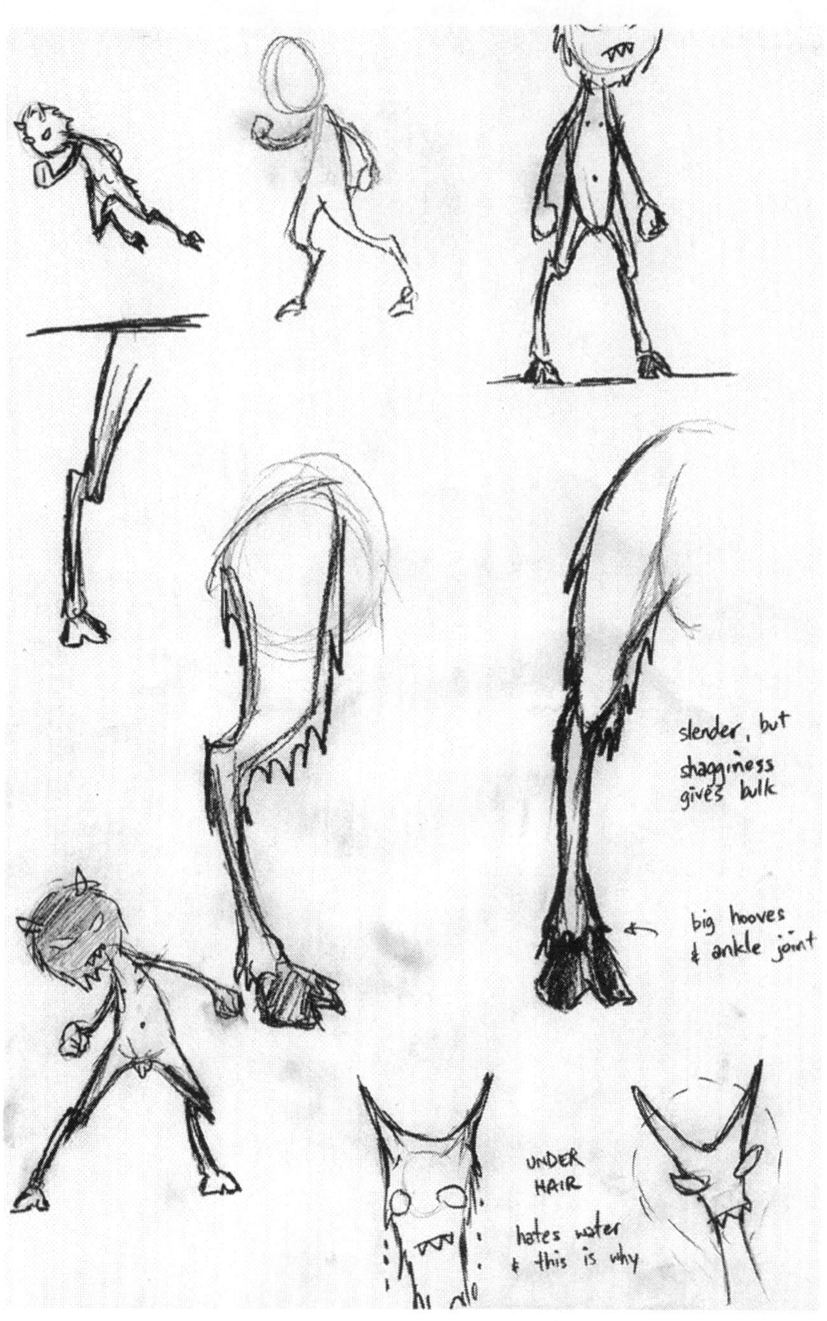
slender, but
shagginess
gives bulk
big hooves
& ankle joint
UNDER
HAIR
hates water
& this is why

HAHAHAHAHAHAHAHAHA etc.

pointy ?
itchy
itchy

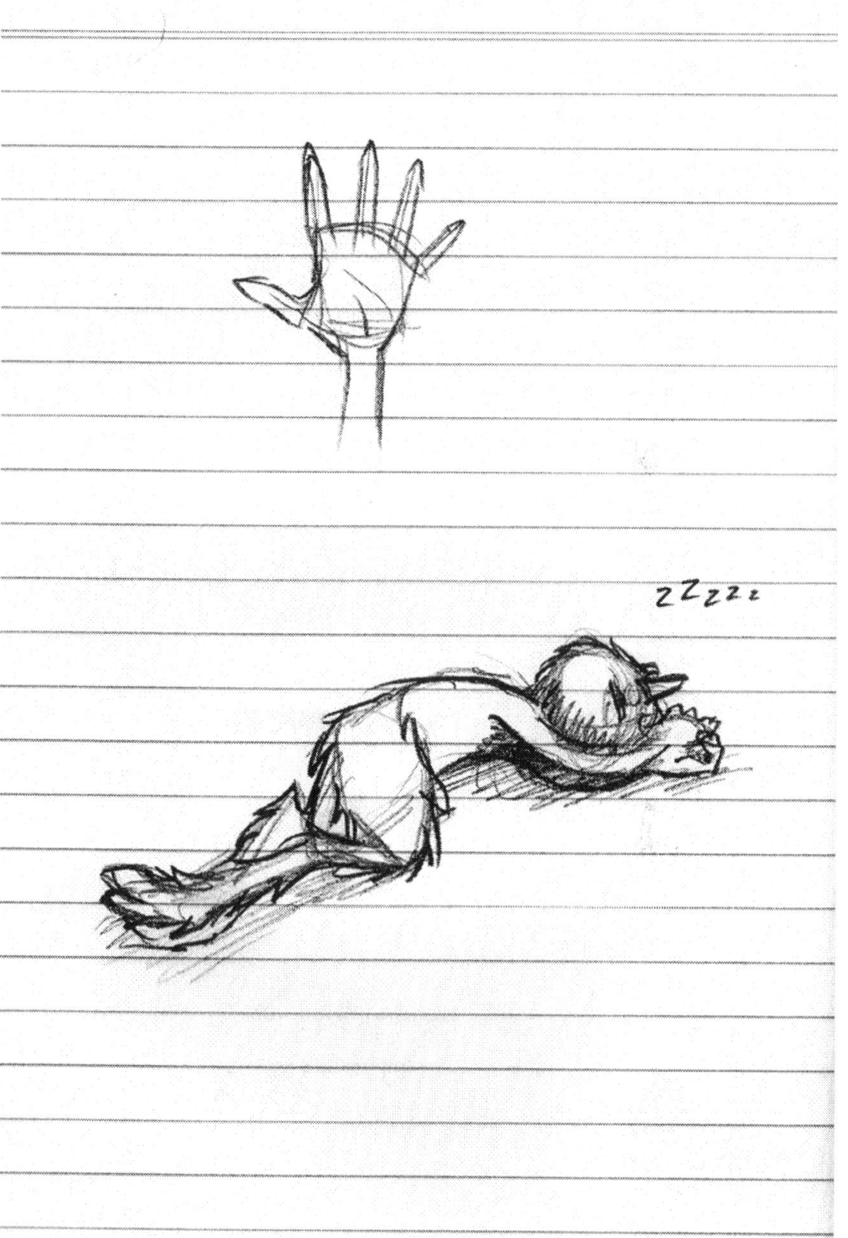
zZzzz

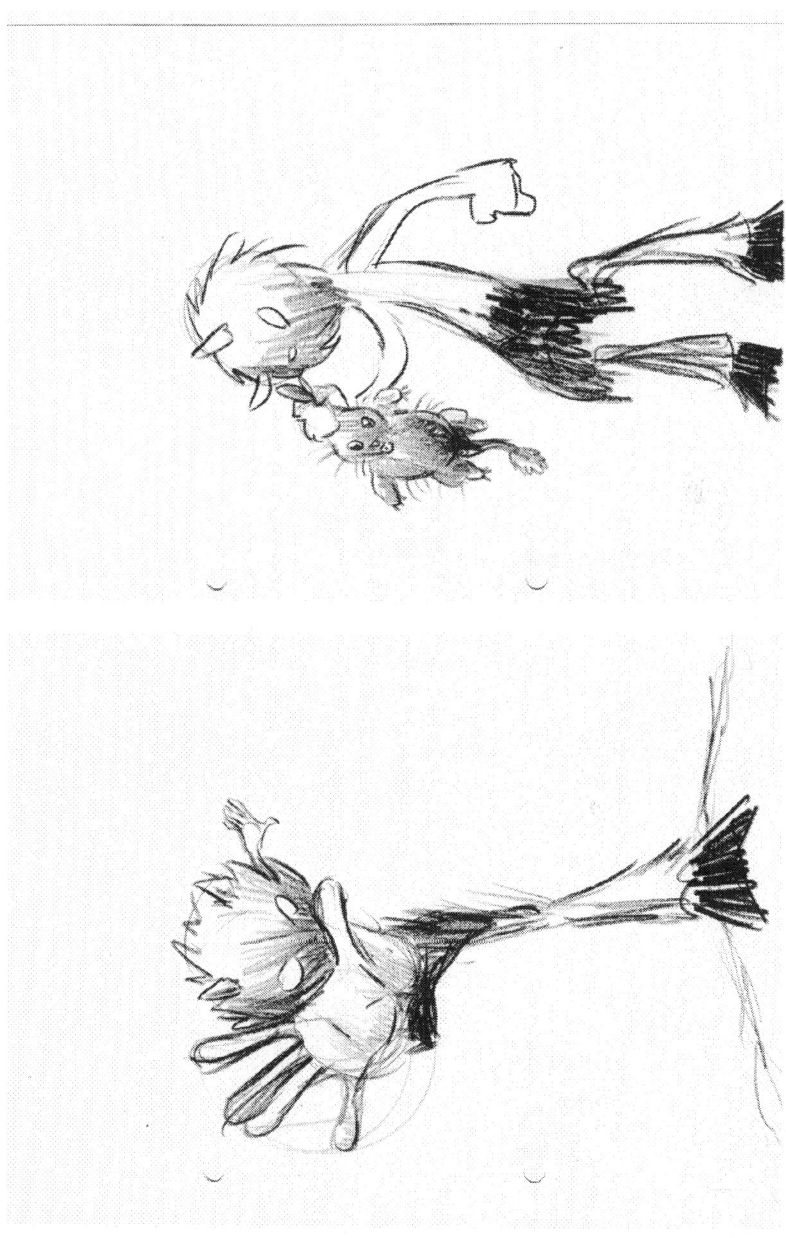

SQUIK!

THE AULD SAGE

The Auld Sage was created as a kind of gentle forest giant who is old and wise. The archetypal wise old man on a mountain top.

At the time I was designing him, popular cartoon characters always seemed to be in-your-face loud, hyperactive and insane. Even Bingbong had some measure of that OTT silliness. The more I was drawn into developing the world of Brackenwood, the more I wanted to do something different. Surely audiences would someday tire of characters that simply scream humour into you, right?

In developing the Auld Sage character, I was aiming for the opposite. Slow, gentle, almost boring but with a lot going on under the surface. Not to mention his nakedness.

His story developed but he remains a deep mystery. Even today, I'm the only one who knows exactly who he is. I haven't even written it all down so if I die before his story is told, it'll die with me. So when I say he is without doubt the deepest and most complex of all the Brackenwood characters, you'll just have to trust me for now.

WATER LOLLIES

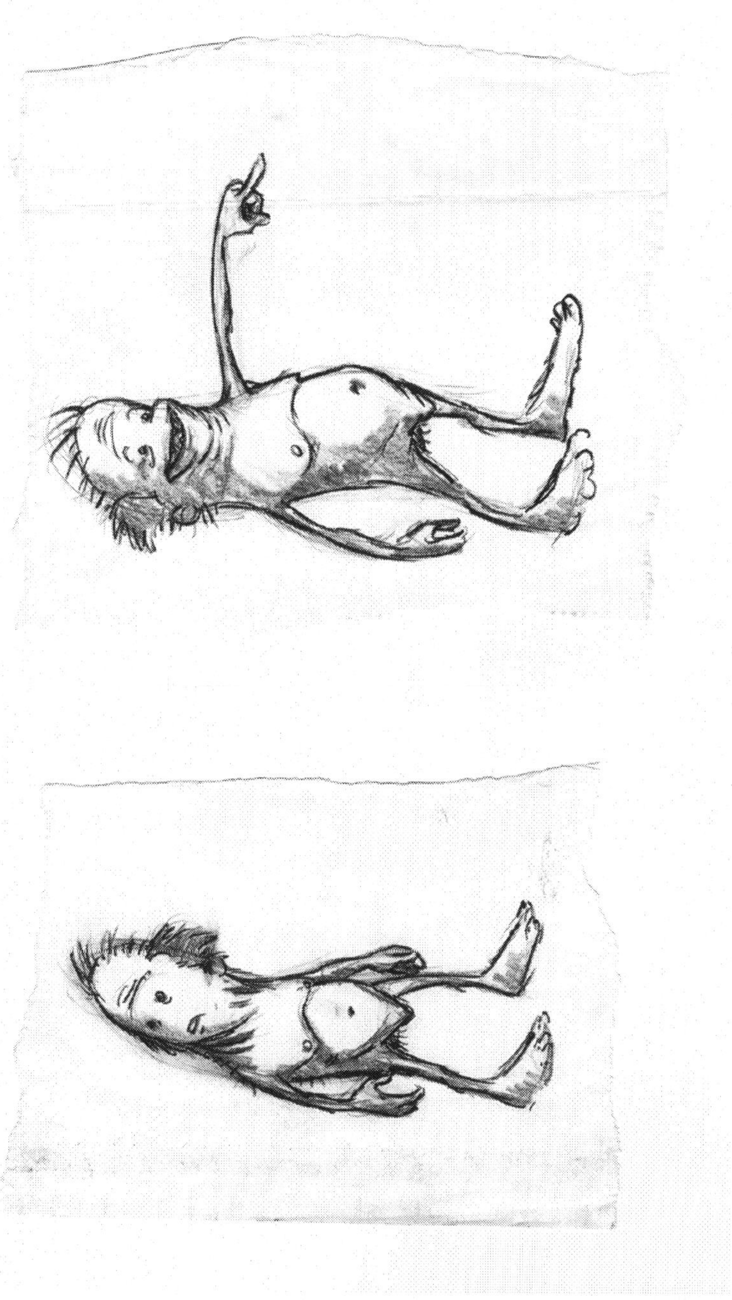

OOWA

LEMONEE WEE

I'll admit it. Lemonee Wee was a name first. How I came up with the name, I'll leave to your imagination. Perhaps I'll tell you over a beer some day.

My earliest sketches of a pudgy young witch in rags are sadly (thankfully?) nowhere to be found. One day having coffee with a friend and colleague, David Wilkinson, I asked his advice in designing this character. He sketched a very cartoony design that I instantly fell in love with.

It's badly smudged but I was amazed to find David's original sketch of Lemonee Wee and her house. I couldn't possibly leave it out, so here it is on the facing page!

The designs on pages 49 and 50 are mine, expanding on David's design and getting my own feel for it.

In 2009's 'The Last of the Dashkin', I completely changed her design to be more in line with my own style, but David's original design is how fans were first introduced to her. As such, it has a special place in Brackenwood's history book.

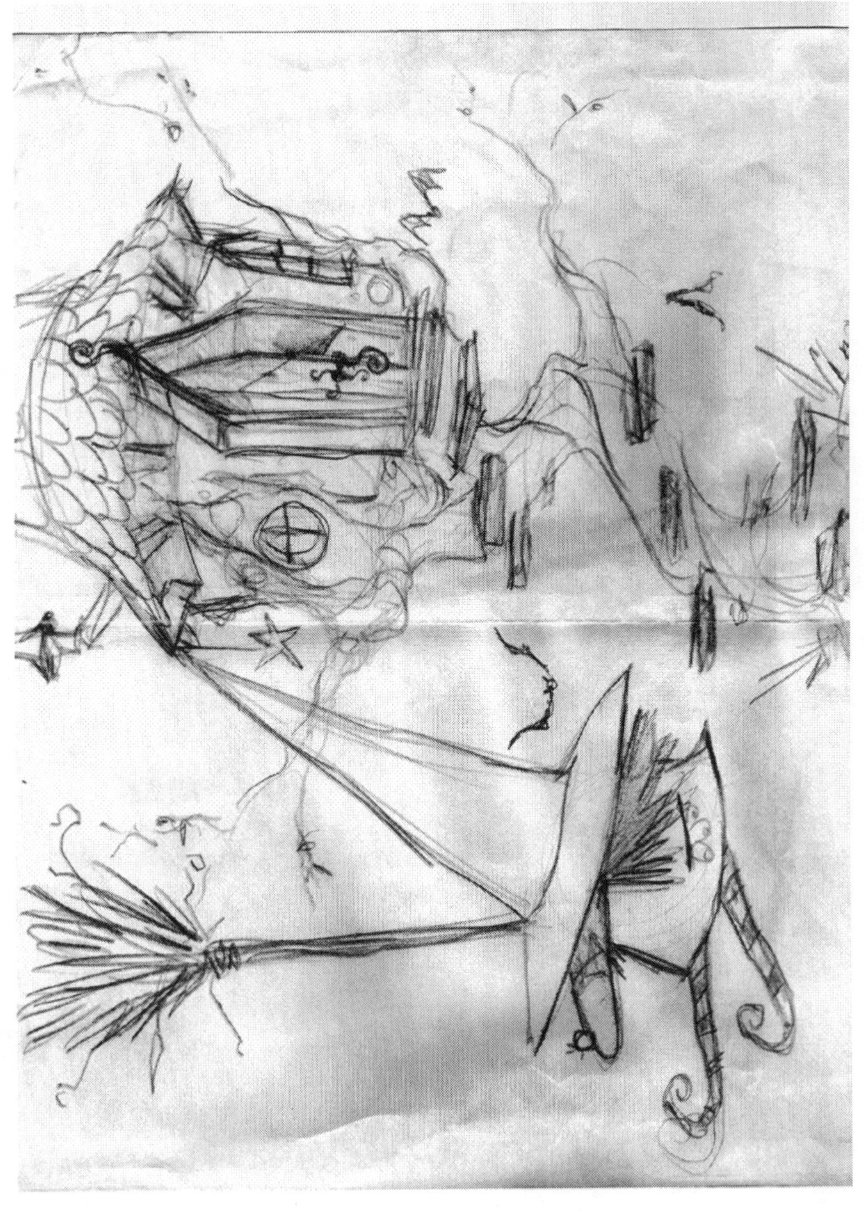

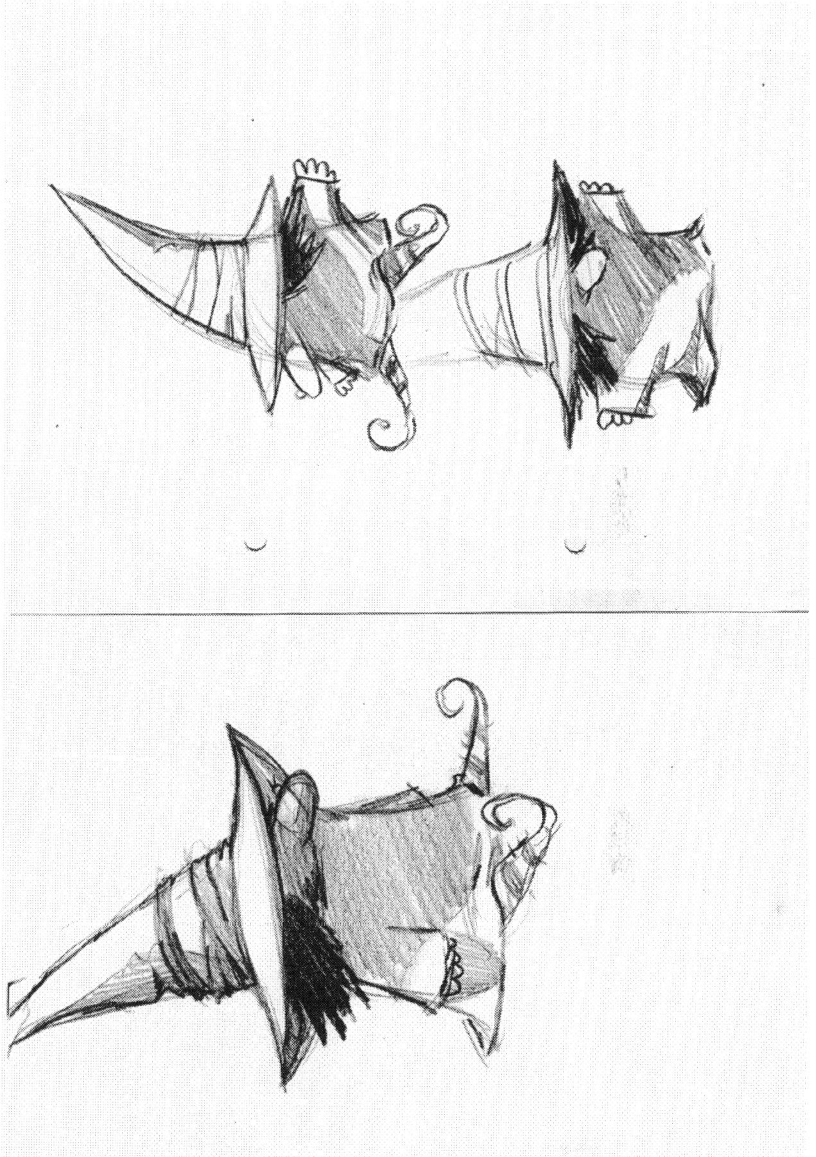

FATSACK

The hapless sack of digestive juices was created with the sole purpose of being beaten up in Bitey's first movie.

At the time I had no idea how beloved he was to become with fans. Even today, I receive emails from people asking about the "farty yellow thing".

Some people have referred to him as a bird, others point out the similarities to "peeps", which are marshmallow Easter treats in the USA.

We don't have those here in Australia but when I think back and wonder what inspired his design, it's probably the weird creature Gary Oldman keeps under his desk in the Luc Besson film 'The Fifth Element'. That terrified looking bag of smooth skin. A sack of fat.

Fans on the Brackenwood forum named him Jiblet and thereafter he made appearances in most subsequent episodes.

The first designs of fatsack were like some generic mammal with ears, claws, teeth and nipples! The sketches on page 54 are closer to the final design that fans know and love.

POOT

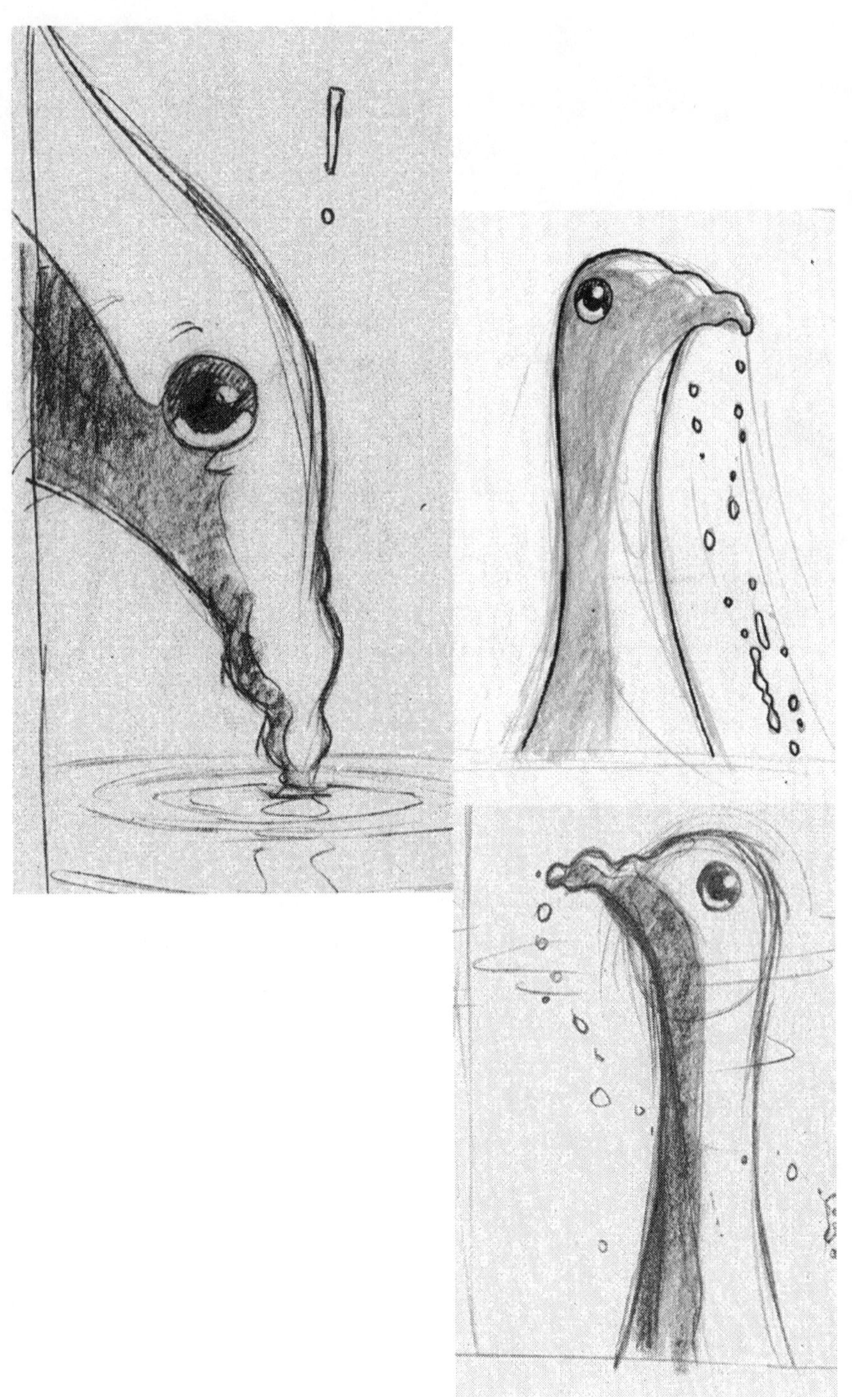

THE YUYU

When I was a kid I'd see these little shadowy people dancing towards me from the corner of the room. I was convinced I could hear them coming for me as I was falling sleep. They had a low droning chant, "YUyu YUyu YUyu YUyu.." If I hid under my pillow or even covered my ears, they'd get louder and I could almost feel them crowding in over me.

As I grew older the Yuyu stayed with me. I became accustomed to their chant and occasionally even bid them goodnight as I drifted off. I still hear them today if I listen hard enough, even now as I type this.

As an adult, I recognise it as the sound of my own heartbeat. Even so, those little shadowy shapes and faces are etched into my mind.

My designs of individual Yuyu are based on those early memories. However, after designing the Yuyu cloud my pride was smashed when a friend told me they looked like the smoke monster in a television series called 'Lost'. I'd never seen the show so I searched online. Sure enough, it was identical and I was devastated.

I'm still tweaking various Brackenwood designs though, so the Yuyu are on that "rework" list.

PROWLIES

I'm immensely proud of the prowlies design because I feel it's truly unique. I worked and reworked several versions of the creature, which I've included here. You'll see early prowlies with beaks, legs, prowlies that resemble frogs, owls and squirrels. In the end though as you know, it's the dark grey amphibious design that won for its character and simplicity.

★ Movement

arms: walk jump turn creep climb

head: full range, i.e turn, roll, tilt, etc.

tail: like possum.. grabs things, coils, balance
can be used as weapon &
sometimes used as third leg

MISC CREATURES

Along the way, each episode has called for various incidental creatures. Not all of them went through a full design process. Some of them were created on the day that I sat down to animate the scene.

Here are a few random creature designs that never made it into any episode.

ABOUT THE AUTHOR

I started my career in 2D animation in 1993 when I landed a traineeship with Walt Disney Television Animation Australia.

A decade later I was the effects director of the same studio. But it was my personal website that was gaining recognition. I was contributing to books and conferences on the use of Flash for animation, my own animated web shorts were winning awards and gathering a loyal following of fans and I was turning down work offers every other day.

In 2004 I finally decided it might be time to go independent. Scary at first, it seemed to go very well and here we are, eight years later in the month of the apocalypse, 2012 and I manage to make ends meet.

My main goal in life is to own a quiet acre or two with goats and build a modest stone tower in the image of Bitey Castle. My Brackenwood series is, and always has been some paving of the road toward that goal.

I currently live in Leura, Blue Mountains, NSW, Australia with my favourite person, Jeanette. I've seen UFOs, I like nature and also knives.

Made in the USA
Charleston, SC
24 March 2013